THE PROPERTIES OF BREATH

JEAN HANFF KORELITZ

The
Properties
of Breath

BLOODAXE BOOKS

Copyright © Jean Hanff Korelitz 1988

ISBN: 1 85224 069 5

First published 1988 by
Bloodaxe Books Ltd,
P.O. Box 1SN,
Newcastle upon Tyne NE99 1SN.

Bloodaxe Books Ltd acknowledges
the financial assistance of Northern Arts.

Typesetting by Bryan Williamson, Manchester.

Printed in Great Britain by
Bell & Bain Limited, Glasgow, Scotland.

For
Dorothy Ruth Hanff Zabin
and
Ann Dorothy Zabin Korelitz

Acknowledgements

Acknowledgements are due to the editors of the following publications in which some of these poems first appeared: *Encounter, The Honest Ulsterman, Kalliope* (USA), *Other Poetry, Orbis, P.E.N. New Poetry 1* (Quartet Books, 1987), *Poetry Durham, Poetry Ireland Review, Poetry Now, Poetry Review, Poetry Wales, The Rialto, The Scotsman, Spare Rib,* and *Writing Woman.*

I am also grateful to the Harper-Wood Studentship Committee (St John's College, Cambridge), the Marguerite Eyer Wilbur Foundation and the Dartmouth College General Fellowships Committee.

Contents

I. *Descending the Lung*

Hand over hand, we inch. Our grips
are fine hairs, moving in their tides. We sink
from rung to coated rung, until
it broadens out: a landscape, arcing
to the edges of the body. Looking
over shoulders we can see it: lung,
translucent mine, its dim. We cannot
move our feet for the mire the smoke makes.

Bottles
(for my father)

Brittle as a mass grave: we
are digging out the browns
and blues and holding them
against the temperamental sun.

Mother says there is a fine line
between antiques and junk, but we
have always walked it, with furtive
trips to the garbage pile, apprehending
what treasure she has thrown
to some uncaring trashman,

and taking our shovels to the hill
behind our house, where with digging
we can learn the former tenants
had been often constipated, often drunk.
We wash their citrate of magnesium,
their clorox, with a reverence
for that perhaps-old glass,

the carved leaves, faces growing
from beneath old dirt, years
of the hill behind our house pressed in, and leave them
drying on the grass, redeemed
to sunlight, empty
of their wine and soap, and fat
with air.

The Fruit Trees

Fresh from mail-order, they arrive:
impoverished on the doorstep, sticks
with their kinetic bases wrapped
in burlap: peach, plum, pear.

In the rise at the edge of the meadow, we plant
them. Father, our aim
is the improvement
of the property, or something
else, unnameable: the tired hand
that spreads out, laboring its upward
birth, explosions made of fruit, as angry
as first gasps of air.

Years they stick, immovable.
We water diligent, and turn
the earth; we wrap
them from the flies and wait. We're waiting
for the fold of generations, years to close
upon themselves like oriental fans, collapsing
daughter into father into earth.

They disappoint us, in their way; the plum
will bear no plums; the peach
shows little balls of fuzz the caterpillars
get. The pear's
our only hope, but we have pruned
our hoping: stillborn, first,
it had refused us. When you wanted
to uproot it I said no, a logic
only children hold against
the obvious: 'Don't pull it. It will grow.'

And in the years past waiting, so it did:
a thief like creep, it coiled
its ancestor until
that fell away, then grew, then reached
my father's height, then mine.

If we have failed, what's left
is what we do not speak of. There is pleasure
enough in the garden; what was planted
will survive us. Knowing this,
my father asks, now, to be buried
beneath those fruit trees.

My Grandfather and the Dog

He has been dead three days, or gone
at least. One night
we drive the roads to look
along their ditches five miles
from the house, find nothing.

Age, I think. And strange
how they have aged uneven, one of them
with hair gone white around the muzzle, marking
lines like thought along the crown, and one
grown finer, stroke
by stroke, each leaving
thinner traces of what's still
called handsome, what we mark
in photographs: on shipboard, or
in breeches, carrying my mother's mother in a field.

The workings of one
muscle in his chest; I am
well versed in this and watch
for signals: breath
or perspiration, anything
like strain. In deference, I
become as pliant, let
the late sun move us quietly
across the patio.

Later, we will walk
the woods as quiet, looking
for the dog. This Sunday's
Easter and the great-
grandchildren will disperse
here for the eggs he'll hide in brush
and under trees. I'm hoping
none of them will find him, cold
in his expected death, stiff
and unrisen in the undergrowth.

North

Last night in your car we barreled northward, car
heat insulated from the outside: wild
we cornered curve on curve of Yukon scene, we let it stretch
to left, to right, a tundraed swamp, uncloaked
and almost frightening, almost
euphoric as helium.

Wood burns better here; you come
from Florida where the Confederate trees won't
light. In this cabin it's so simple even I
can make it blaze, and tame it,
write before it. You can split
log on log of northern wood, so heady
with that skill you brandish axe and threaten
like some Lizzie Borden of a blue-
jeaned man, dark-haired and frigid
as the white sunlight.

When you leave to hike, I leave too,
photographing foliage all the way down
to the creek and turning back
to fire-sit the cabin.
There is no tea or coffee.
We have fouled the milk with ashes.
There are only the wood walls, and my strong fire,
and outside, through the skylight, the hard north.

The IRA Visits Us in Newry

A stop for tea at the border, tea
and cakes and a quick
smoke. In the holding-pen of the parking
lot, we've long
since finished when the train itself
lights up, a long one. We can only

watch and have it blown black
in our faces, from the windows
where our faces would have been.

Moscow

Sometimes it takes years, the wait
between our applications, and the State's
responses often quite ridiculous: 'Your aged
parents would not join you, should you leave
for Israel. We must, you understand, preserve
the unity of family.' Or this:
'Your wife's research is vital
to the military interests of the state.' She works
on chicken embryos.

And afterwards, we know these frigid looks
along the grey ice of our street, lost places
at the University, demotion. We apply again, of course.

Mornings. Through intrusive static, we
can just make out the BBC, and crouch
here, steadying strong
coffee on our thighs, the strain
to hear obscuring everything.

Munich

Wolfgang poses by this statue
of a down-and-out. My click
is sudden like the air's bite, as exclusive. Here,
he points, is where the Reich held rallies. Here
is our Bavaria, huge
in darkness over the Oktoberfest
field. I'm led around; my feet
are not my own. I sign
my traveler's checks in the bank, rehearsing
my own name, the teller's balding eye.

In the morning we make the awkward drive to the camp,
stilled in silence. I want
to apologise, oddly, can't think why.
American soldiers walk their wives
and tape decks past the photographs
of medical research (What pressure
does a Jew's ear need to shatter?). Then we file
past grey holes where the barracks were and down
by the memorials in deference to what's died.
Near the ovens, there are signs who warn us
not to smoke, fire extinguishers
hanging the walls.

The Merely Good

There is this smell to evening, and this pattern: how
a pine branch dips the river here and parts it
like your loss from the reluctance of a memory.

You were in the mirror when I came to visit, eyeing me
through smogs of disbelief. It is the only
thing I can recall without a withering: the light
when you had turned to me, released
your razor like a sigh into the sink and pulled
me, hard against you, awkward.

Too safe for me, that pure thing
in the letters you had sent, your clumsy poems,
devoted. I had sought
no supplicant, was out
for something made of darkness,
wind. The merely good
was boring. How
can I explain this? Brad,

when mother said you'd died, and rolled
untended from that crumpled
car, my own regrets turned worthless. Now
the night wind blows them back
in my face, the dark evening smells, the waste.
I did not understand; I did not know
the car would turn, would crumble
you like confessions.

16 May 1961

My mother's last untroubled words
before the gas
are these: I will not have a son
named David.

The day of my appearance
is the day my father's due
on the voting block
of Lenox Hill Hospital. Their votes

accompany my party down the corridor:
the obstetrician's and the anesthesiologist's.
One takes my father to one
side, and tells him: Burt, I can deliver

only one of you – yourself, your kid. Your choice.
We're all of us enraptured
by my slow unraveling between her gassed-out
thighs, the obstetrician's 'Pink her up!',

my father, me, the both of us, inducted fine
(though neither knew it at the time).

Severn Bridge

Given a chance, that sliver of bare
space between his bottom
teeth might grow till it accommodates
the world. At two o'clock

they board Slattery's Bus
in Tralee, stuck leg to leg. By ten
they've grown distinct and contact
is, if anything, a grimy
fingertip, the blunt heel of his leather
shoe, or the unkind
disturbance of the air
that silence makes.

At five the sun is up near Severn Bridge.
The drowsy gaze
of horses and a vague
throb in her left thigh, slowly
coming to consciousness. His tired
voice behind her back:

Severn Bridge is one of the longest
in the world, but not the longest.

Digging the Unused Lung

What comes up I hold
against the light. I stoop
for handfuls of this stuff, the blurred
necessity of clearing it: the unused lung,
its surfaces of stillness
over years, their odd corruptions
of unwillingness to speak. To break
that film and feel
for what might live in its thick
dark's a kind of love. Days now,
and nights I'm here, intolerant
of world events and other people, dredging
it to usefulness: unrealised
breath, or tongue. I won't know
anything until I'm done.

Communion

The plane's a drunk, and lurching
to a pattern neither
of us recognises – wheeze
or gasp, its roll
across the dark with wings
against the belly of its body, and we sit,
accustomed in our one seat, two
legs crossed against the elements, the dark
of the betweens.

Time: they bring us
food for syncopated appetites; we eat
for two – one bite
of an expatriate sandwich and one glass
of disembodied wine. At last,

in this crawlspace above the countries, we begin
our integration – slow, two lungs
into a master and two rivers
of a pulse combining quietly, unsafe: one file
of poems in the aircraft's belly and one body
in its cluttered spine, no country

and no weight. We are so light
that currents scatter us about like jumping beans
who never land. One drink
in mid-flight equals two
on earth, as any traveler
might well discover.

II. *Burning the Property*

Smoke wakened us: the field
sloping up to the stone wall filled
with it, the filaments
of our neighbor's grasses flying.
Shovels and boots: our heels
brought his seedling flames back
to the earth, making them
black ash, a thick
scar at the field's rim.

Later, when the smoke had stilled, our neighbor
scattered ashes from his cigarette. He stubbed it
in the black, remarking
that it hardly mattered now. His chest
expelled itself. The property
would be more fertile, he decided, for that burn.
We eyed his steaming streaks, those tumors
on the lung of his slopes.

Passion

Home in the darkness again, my breath
is the same as the air, thick as the conspiracy
of your two doors locked.
Sullen through streets; your voice
becomes indistinguishable from the whoosh
of cars, even in this dead hour. I have forgotten
all the rudiments now, the expectations
of to sleep, to wake ready
for what may happen; all blurs
here in my thin bed, the night gone thick
from breathing what I do not remember.

A medical report says:
nudge a fetus at ten weeks and there is pain, a flail
of unformed limb, an underwater cry.
And here is your pencil, proving it, coming
out of the dark to make a wave in my poetry,
and there is no control; my arms are moved, my legs
propelled through clogged and self-important
streets to this tyrannical door – unborn.
There is only the drift from crest to crest
with whatever I presume to want ungraspable
in the wet. Time distorts. I age writhing.

Nights are most orderly; there is nothing to achieve.
Even the imagined mouth to what of me
quickens and churns breeds nothing; I lie dryly,
examine ceiling, wall, window.
The clock, about its business,
announces passion, passion.

What Is Worthy of Regard

Your rug is shedding on me, white
hairs on the black
of my legs, where black
hair grows, where there is a lift
and twist and I twine
arms and angle my face.

In your rooms there is much
worthy of regard: the rain
out your courtyard window I don't
give a damn for, but in here, in a chair
that curves you, forcing
words through fingers, meeting
anything but my eyes – this
makes a difference.

From the kitchen, your little room
of secret things, you bring out pewter,
cheese, a quail egg. I'm incapable. I'm shocked
to a lull by the rivers
your long fingers make, and wondering
what marks they leave.

The volume's ponderous. You smile
in a straight line and play obtuse.
Why won't you name this? Even I
with white-stained legs and angled face, can name
this pull: the strain, what reels from walls,
what hollows out my palms.

Smoke

The air is full of leaves; each day
the smoke moves through my lungs, a body inflated
from the aftermath of burning, legs a puff.
The heat runs off in gulps. I walk here,
past heaps of the season, feeding off fumes
to the chilling air.

Night sweats: this is not a dream,
perhaps, though possibly some incubus
in the rippling. Something
hard's behind me; something warm has pressed
me pliant, flattening and flattering, thickening
the air with its breath. We don't bother
to make up the bed or part
the curtains or go out for more food.

Day and night become indistinguishable.
Our bodies grow hair in the dark and we let it grow.
One of us stops going to the toilet. The same
record plays again and again. Slowly, certain
as an illness, this small room
begins to fill with smoke, until
there is no difference, just
the running of a slow
blood well in me to mark
the time, another waste down my thighs.

A window cracks with light; our tongues
come unstuck as the smoke thins and the cold
air rushes in, waking
me, thickly, wet.

Oedipus Comes Home

Womb is where he lives; the déjà vu
on entering, familiarity of doors.

Our generations wrap him up like palace gates; he polishes
the stone steps of our thighs with his tongue, breathing
names like a fetal whisper: lover, angel, kicking
to get back inside. But we

are only legs that open, breasts
for the burrowing between, the darkening
of eyes: we are only women, bridals
towards diminishment, our caves and stones.

His feet may swell from grief; he cannot place
what's vaguely reminiscent at the breast.

In Sleep

Asleep you might be more yourself; the low
hum of it can hover and diminish
you, your features. Now
you reach for what is unused
space in this dark around
the body. What
do you imagine touching – something
hard, the reassurance of defined
rock? Or the blur
of hair, skin, wet I've taken
to this corner of the room where I
am crouched, and watch?

O, your mouth says, O. If we talked,
we two, in sleep, what would we tell?
Awake, the muscles of our tongues conspire, spar.

Loving Janus

His breath might fill
the house, if I let it. Already
it's wormed the floorboards up
to my unsubtle attic bed, its suck
like some unlikely halo in the dark. My blanket's
insubstantial to the rasp.

Or: he might, himself, ascend, to touch
with one finger the jut
of my hip and wish me luck
with the rest of my life. In loving

Janus I have come to tolerate
such things as these and every bit
expect, by morning, to have found
him in his normal place, his breath in state
around him: sitting
the doorway, surveying
my perpetual goings and comings.

Birth Control

I carry the eggs.

The mud's what incubates, accepting
our feet with sounds like the sucking of mouths.
What you carry up this hill is obstacle: a brown bag
sullen with potatoes, cans, with things
you needn't nurture. As we climb
you shift them worryless between
the angles of your elbows, wrists. Beside you
or behind I'm stepping, conscious
as a membrane, eggs to chest, protecting
what is possible.

A disparity of sentiment.
You may have the weight but it's my
breath coming faster and more futile. I'm unfit,
you say. Your face cuts hard against this wind; your cans
sound the surface of what's between us:
barrier, barren. We
have nothing in common, you say.

But why are there eggs in my arms? Each morning
I birth my rubber cradle in the bath
and your dead filaments fly out, disappointed.
We disappoint each other, do we not?

Our feet want sinking; the frail
things I hold want realisation.
Over the clank of breathing, puff
of metal can I hear denial and renounce. In my arms

something riots, quietly.

33

B

What Gets Broken

'I feel you are being somewhat naïve, Rofrano.
I can imagine who she is. I find her charming.'
   The Marschellin (over her shoulder
   to Octavian) in *Der Rosenkavalier*

With such fanfare has he found
someone his own age that, in a quick response,
she's thrown a plate, articulating sharpened
points around the room. It has been coming. Years,
across the twin peaks of their backs
in bed, she's known he'd leave her: this
seems no less sudden.

It's thick winter. Neither
has been sleeping well, and somewhere
in the country house *Der Rosenkavalier*
is playing on their stereo, till
one of them has lost
their patience, thrown it to the iron
gratings of the fireplace. It sends
its shards, their filaments of silence up
the chimney to the open air, abandoning
each room to their untempered voices.

If this were opera they might then
consider, say, the respiration
of the wine, the summer's pesto. As it is,
he'll crouch behind the broad
bowl of her back, and hide
there. She'll be left
another plate to break, a bottle
leveling itself.

Brund

Each day gropes colder. What we see
from the window first fills
then empties with snow. The scene
is limp, finally, an aftertaste.
Each night we leave a wicker basket
by the front door for the landlord
to fill with wood. My fires won't light.
Is there nothing I can do for you?
What are my most useful parts?
Mouth? Or breast?

One of us does not trust the inexplicable.
For one of us, explanation
is irrelevant, a dead skin
on milk, a disappointed
line of smoke from the firewood.

I need you for this, for warmth.
Nights we burn off the words of the day,
what's coagulated here: space
between us on the bed evaporating
as one of us goes, heated, to the other.
Perhaps, I think, this is all that is left,
this speech of skins our only common tongue. What you call
across to me I believe still, even

now, even after you have left this stone
cottage, this full basket of wood I cannot light.

Tiger Stripes

First day: who will admit
it's not what we'd expected?
In the back of my throat is this couch
with tiger stripes; you choose
a room upstairs for the work
you will not do. We growl from hunger.
I bring you a first meal. I learn
the patterns of your pacing.

Days pass: we figure
ways to cut. Your hair ends
sharpen in the sunlight as you walk me
among cows, between the edges
of your body, like an experiment
who will not realise.

When there is no comfort: we cook
what can't be said. I swallow only
what your hand has touched because
it will no longer touch me: your sauté
is a caress, your slow boil
the diffusion that our mouths won't make.

Last morning: I have lost
my appetite. You're leaving me
with seven bottles of good wine, an unlit
fire, half a pack
of your Gitanes. Who will admit
this was expected? We
have given up to failure, everything:
the undone work, the stripes
where we have drawn out pain, our tongues
a famine when they touch goodbye.

A Dream of Scorpions

Brown not black, the color of an earthen
mound to mark a burial. It spread
its scales against a white
wall, eyeing me.

Quicker than scent, the stun
of disappearance, how it hid itself and how
I found it, after, by its quiet throbs, a sullen
warm at the hip's edge where
it gripped, embedding itself head
first, grabbing flesh, the unused
sting saluting space around it.

I'd been harmed, and steeled, I'd start
to grip it out, avoid
each manic claw, the tail. It broke twice,
burrowed deeper. I dug out
its parts, my fingerfuls of flesh.

Later, I describe it. You're amused.
Brown leather crinkles at your elbows
when you move. I watch it, wondering.
The grey-run black that grows
in silence from the edges of our bodies
moves the air; the hairs along our spines
twitch. Bothered, you inhale
your dark tea, then uncoil
to leave. I watch it, stung, the warm
edge of the pelvis rising
like an opened grave, and you
are in the bone by now, and I
shall never pick you out, entire.

III.   *The Properties of Breath*

These are the patches we circumvent, their pools
of dark. They list the properties of breath:
involuntary, breeding, burned. Tonight
our cigarettes smoke end to end, drawn down
to settle in that dim. What things grow here
we do not tend or till.

Our lungs expel themselves. We trap
what comes up, call it poetry.

Concerning Gorgons

We were the lookalikes: black-haired Greeks gone wild
in Bloomingdales, or thrift stores – to our mothers' shock.
How often I was called by your name, turning
in the street while someone stared,
then rattled, You're not Vicki, are you?

For what it's worth, I did not mind
our being so confused:
in looks, in laughter, politics.   •

Laughing over tea, you puffed
the liquid, drank
the cigarette; you did things
backward of me, that's how alike
we trawled the sidewalk, then – two Gorgon sisters, crazy
with their hair and voices, sharing
that single derisive eye and wishing
they were men, or gay, or poets.

Snorkeling with My Father

My fear was this: to dive and fill
the black tube, knowing
the water would force its passage: mouthpiece
to a gut of swimming things too small
or quick for eyes. I'd hang
to the surface while you'd dart
at shells or rocks. I'd rub my legs
and arms to free them of what crept
or clung, counting
the strokes to safety, dying for land.

This is my apology, father, for the skin
so quick to become cold, for the fear
of things that crept, but most
for swimming back to shore
that one day, touching
your shoulder, saying
with my hands and eyes, I'm going in,
I'm going back, but knowing
it was not enough, and leaving
with my quiet doubt you'd understood.

When, on the beach, safe
in the finite sand, my mother said, Where's Daddy? I
was nonchalant, and when
the fishing boats went crazy offshore and you stumbled
from the water, crying, thinking, How
can I tell Ann? I would not comfort you. My skin
crept. Shaking, you spread shells at my feet.

A Pearl

Always, we left Liberty
on the right, her acid
green skirts trailing
the Hudson, my father
motioning: 'A gift
from the French.' I'd
imagine it gift-wrapped.

All told, the distance
from our dark East
Side apartment to the waste
of Coney Island was two
tunnels and the wretched
West Side docks. We'd home in
on the grey streets bordering
the Boardwalk.

Anything that might have drawn us
was instead drawn up
for the winter: water-pistol
shoots in frozen streams behind
their grates, the goldfish stiff
in dirty ice, the Hurricane
and Cyclone facing off
across an empty lot, their girders
moving in the unkind wind.

The only pearl in all of this
was Nathan's, pouted at year-
round by the bare-assed
Coppertone girl from her billboard
across the street: its stalls and stalls
of clams. With our quota,
then, of Cherrystones, we might retire

to some sheltered place: a doorway, or
the phone booth where, one day, he drew
from between the cold flesh and his teeth
an irritant, which might have been
sand, or might once
have been sand.

The point around which the world
gathers is as humble
as that, as what we stared at, what
he left, and what I hope
still to reclaim as spare
change from some public
phone, checking even now the coin
returns to feel
for it: its fingered
surfaces, its thick
resilient core.

The Sounds from the Stairs

The bumps in the road as we drove here; the bumps
in Shelby's voice as she talks about her son.
She cries on the back stairs while I wash
out the dishes from dinner and pretend
not to hear it, the sounds from the stairs,
the way the pain runs down her throat.

Beams run the ceiling; this house
is not new. It's carved for a weekend son:
the fishtank, the little bed
I sleep in tonight, an oversized
and awkward visitor who does not understand
her grief of gestation, the ache of her womb.

Shelby telephones women; they listen.
I write on the rug, autonomous
on my flat belly, deflect the hurt
while I can. You should not marry, she says,
quietly from the stairs.

Steaming

The library is steaming, heat
licked as some old barn gone brittle
with electric storms. The walls
cave inward from us. Someone

smokes. I turn my pages. Everyone
drinks tea at four
o'clock. At six I watch you coming in. You melt
the doorway, tread the carpet white hot. Heat
runs from the walls. My cheeks catch flame.

Outside, on the library steps, the windows
glow out gold to us, lighting, in a half way,
my face, steaming your grandfather's glasses.

In Dreams Begin Responsibilities

Young then, she dreamt herself
hunched in a room too shallow
to accommodate her shoulders:

limp flowers on the walls, a bed
unnatural in size, a body
on the bed. The weight of its white

limbs made a furrow into which
she burrowed her forearms, lifting what
was a mirror of herself, surprising,

after all, in lightness. To carry it
through that keyhole of a door, the mouse-
run of a corridor meant carrying

herself as an offering in a bundle
of sticks. Edging through another door
she found her dead mother, calmly

sitting with folded hands. The shadowed
half of her face, unfinished knitting
in her lap, a leaden quality in that familiar
voice: Oh yes. I can see that's you.

Not that any of it shocked her, when she thought
it out. Or frightened her. Instead
she left her husband of eight years.
Now I can laugh, she says. Her white

hair catches the light. Oh yes. That was me.

Apple Doll

What is now my head was once
the darkest apple in Clara's orchard.
No one might suggest
the true motive of its pigment, or
the split spur of its stem. There
but for the sudden shift of what is now
my gaze I hung for the whole
of autumn, then fell
irresistibly to earth. Winter was my season
for changes as, over months, I aged
inward, hardening in spirit as
in shell, my outer
edges straining towards my core.

These are my eyes: two knob-ends
of pins implanted here as I began
my shrink. Empty wire circles
focus my gaze on the world. This
is my mouth: a curved knife-wound collapsing
into numb and toothless happiness. New yarn
is the static covering of my hair.

In the end, it was my color
chose my role. Now, in my domestic's
cloth, I serve and smile endlessly. Only,
as an afterthought or oversight,
my hands and feet are the white
of old nylons: a second
treasured pair kept back
when patriotism claimed all Clara's others
for the effort overseas.

Ashes
(for Beatrice McHugh, 1892-1982)

When you became dead, pale
lipped as the angel you had wanted
to grow into, I kissed
before two tired nurses each side
of the silent face, the mouth
that had explained so carefully what God
was, what love was, in Irish
tones unbroken over ninety years.

Walking home in the first swells of New York
summer, I was stunned
with it, fermented with the smells
of having waited, the formaldehyde. I made
from your old room a box-filled dead place, dead
as what was laid out in the Catholic
custom, ready for the pale
and blond relations of your other family, and they
were kind to me. They sat with me inside the unfamiliar
church and listened while the priest
who had not known you waved
the incense, mispronounced your name.

Once it was a day called Ash Wednesday, and your legs
had no strength for the kneeling, you said. I came here
as a supplicant and knocked
the altar like a front door. When someone
heard me, I could tell he saw my bones
and coloring were not the Trinity, not sweet
like Christian children, already my dark moods
scented. But he gave me what I'd come for: filtered
ashes in the envelope I'd brought, what blessing
or what holiness they signified, and I
ran home to you and brushed them on the pale
skin, marking with what love I still protect
for you, and mourn you with, almost huge as God's.

Wishbone

Outside the back room off the kitchen, waiting
by the crack of your door as night stilled
through our apartment, as cars slowed outside
but did not stop, I'd listen for the breath
that heaved through you, that rocked you back
against blankets, over and over, letting
the sound reach me, rest me, let me wade
back shaking to my own bed.

By morning you were certainly alive, and waking me
with admonitions of lateness and weather, having walked
like cotton through my room and bathroom, across the dark
boards of the dining room as they creaked, announcing
what small weight you were, what vast importance.

There is no place free of you in our home: the bed
you breathed in, or the kitchen, heating rice,
even my parents' bedroom where you found me
kissing a college boy. I near nine months without
your brittle face glowing to mine, the offer of dollars
for taking away to school, for buying a dress.
No poem encompasses what there was, what has been lost;
no memory's free of the ache for holding you, frail
as the wishbone you would save to break
with me, and let me always win, as if
my wish were more important.

Half Truths, Half Lives

Even now you are wanted for the telling of things:
the dry edge of my tongue in some radioactive room,
the dry edge of your tongue around words.

Heat still comes from it, a fission
heat that melts me, stripping off
my skin. What's left: a core
gone radiant with something
no one names, the feared thing,
what can enter bone by stealth.

But these are only half truths, love, reducing
even as they form in half lives back
to nothing. One more waste
among our many: all these ashes
and activity, so much for the burying.

Dowra

1.

After '65, she never made it back. When Mary died
and Thady was alone in Dowra he would write
to ask her was she fit
for the crossing, but she never was.

When the time came, she would take a place
in the Valhalla Cemetery, half-way
between New York and South Salem.

Driving through it, I would pass the monuments
of the Italians. Further in,
I'd rest her with the Irish:

Dolans and O'Rourkes, a Kerrigan.

2.

Thady's in with these
O'Rourkes and Dolans. Up the road
the farmer, Kerrigan, will show us where the path
drops off as off a cliff. He points us down
a thicket to the cottage, locked
up for its decade, and we peer
through clotted windows at the bed, the blue-
striped crockery we've just now started
to collect, a bird that's half
a skeleton and half
dirt floor.

When we quarrel, as always, it's
for nothing, but you beat
your way back up
to the rented car and slam
yourself inside. I lean against the low
stone wall and find a bottle there, its blue
lip puckering the dirt

and take it up to you,
an offering, until such time as we
might lead it to a place where it might
rest: half-way between New York and South Salem.

Spawn

You fit the hollow of my arm as if
you'd grown there, wandering
spore at the elbow's crook. The ring
of your mouth finds the ring
of my untapped breast, and feeds
on something not
unlike an unstrained
love, or settlement, its fishlike

O's, its domed immunities.

Newbliss

The pillows furrow with his absent
lines; the sheets
rust white. By day
I sort the chaos of his books and rifle
them, dry pages as if
folds of flesh who keep themselves
so closely to themselves and far
off, sending love. What's roused
in me might right itself to frame
his doorway when he crosses it:
the spotless bed, the bookshelf,
stacked with what I've saved.

Though in the end these things are not,
perhaps, substantial, only roofs
we lay across suspicious
walls, anticipating storms. From where
he is, he might know this and telephone
from Newbliss, calling it
'dead center, middle of nowhere', sending love.

Learning the Manual Alphabet

For every breath, there are the ones
not drawn, the unfilled spaces
where two skins converge, their silences. Our tongues
amuse themselves. What language
are we left?

The knots along my edges rise and hammer
at the prison of my teeth for air. But these completions
are within our touch: our unused
words. I spell mine out for you along
your surfaces, with fingers,
telling more than it's advisable to speak.